Private Label Selling Manufacturer's Guide:

Build Your Brand, Produce and Sell Your Own Products Using Amazon FBA Business Model

By

Dale Blake

Table of Contents

3

Private Label Selling For Beginners: Build Your Brand
and Sell Your Own Products Using Amazon FBA
Business Model

By Dale Blake

Introduction

It's not easy to be "an inventor", but there is a market channel that can help you. Private label sales allow you to partner up with one of the major companies in your genre. You do the work, they sell the product as their own, and you benefit from sales volume you probably could never have achieved on your own. There are many factors to consider when deciding whether or not to go down that road, and the choices you make can have a tremendous impact on your ultimate goal of a sustainable system. On one hand, you don't want to undercut your own private sales, again you don't want to handicap yourself with regard to market possibilities, and you also want to do the volume of sales best for your business model. Understanding what private label sales is, and what it is not, will help guide you to making the best decisions for your own personal product or idea.

Chapter 1. What Private Label Means?

Private label is not a very new concept, however treating it as a business model is fairly new. As such, there is much confusion regarding how it works, what it can accomplish, and who is right for that process. It is not the best solution for many types of developers and sellers, however if you fall into the niche category of someone that will benefit, then it can be a tremendous boon to you. Likewise, private label sales may be a great catalyst to your business (if applied in the right markets) and ultimately may prove a springboard for you ultimate success.

Private label sales is essentially the concept of selling your product under someone else's name. Think of it as ghostwriting for inventors and entrepreneurs. You provide the concept, design, manufacturing, and often times even the packaging (more on that later) and they provide powerful channels for marketing, distribution, and high-volume sales. The company you sign with, of course, takes their fair cut of the profits, but the concept of private label is all about numbers. The more product you move, the more money you make.

Private label sales are restricted to any one genre. People have had successful endeavors with anything from health food and sweets, to cosmetics, to whacky new inventions, and especially toys. The key is not the product you're moving, but rather understanding the market you wish to move it in. The popular television show is a prime example of what private label sales looks like (in television show format). One person has a great idea, but no ability to break into a broader market; broader meaning at which ever level they have hit a plateau). They pitch the idea to someone who will either incorporate it into their already established brand, or who will create a brand for it, under the auspices of a larger more capable company.

The larger company benefits from either higher sales, or specific brand recognition, and the individual or small company benefits from broader distribution and higher volume sales. At this level, private label seems pretty direct. There are, however, many factors to consider when deciding whether or not you should go in for private label with your concept or product.

Chapter 2. About The Product

The first step in considering whether or not private label is the path for you, is to consider where in the market your product will fit. Is it something dime-a-dozen? Do you have another water bottle, or your own spin on a flip-flop shoe? If so, you probably don't want to enter the fast-lane, broad stream market of giant stores and discount retailers. The reason is simple. To compete at that level, you need to diminish your profit margins to a hair's breadth, and then make up the difference in an insane sales volume. For most people considering private label sales, this just isn't an option. Even if your water bottle is clever, you can't compete at that level with, let's say, Nalgene. They have already built the product recognition, marketing, manufacturing, and distribution base to swamp all comers. In this case, private label just isn't for you. Rather, try to sell in niche markets where you can charge a little more and offset lower volume with higher margins. You might hit on a small franchise that would be willing to carry your product, or even a national chain that will sell your goods under your own label. If your product is truly better, then eventually you'll be able to hire a contract manufacturer to up your inventory and take a larger market share by either becoming a competitor, or at that point, allowing a large label to incorporate your brand (Ka-ching$$$).

The best products are accessory items. These can be easily co-marketed and the brand that sells your item will know exactly where to place it in the store. For instance, if you have a unique oven-mitt, or vegetable peeler, or cutting board, you private label it to Sunbeam, or Benchmade, or the like, and they sell the item right alongside their other products (many of which are also private labeled). Volume is achieved mostly through traffic, as in this case there likely would not be much marketing.

Another good strategy is to develop a high-quality specialty item. Think mountain biking accessory, baby accessory, or medical accessory. In this case, the company might even undertake a marketing campaign (limited) to inform this higher market set of their new, quality product. There are reasons that these fields are some of the best for private label sales, and we'll explore that soon.

Consider what your product is. Is it an extension of a current product? Is it an accessory product in a niche field? Or is your product something truly novel and unique? A never before seen item. The way you envision your product, and the way you envision your growth, will determine whether or not private label is right for you.

Chapter 3. Is This For You?

This is the number one question you need to ask yourself when considering whether to market your product to a large label. The answer depends on several factors. Before you read on, you should stop and really ask yourself what your goals are (no, more money does not count as a goal). In fact, how carefully to assess your goals and realistic current position will determine, ultimately, how much money you make. So get the dollar signs out of your eyes and really think for a minute.

Are You Building a Brand?

If you plan on developing your own brand name, sooner than later, then private label is not for you. The reasons are plain enough. By marketing your product under another label, you are cannibalizing your own market share. Obviously, the distribution under the other label will be far greater, and likely sales will increase as well...but your own product, that for which your profit margins are significantly higher, will suffer from the competition. If you hope to create your own name in the industry, then it's best to take the slow road and build a name the old fashioned way. It will take much longer, but you have a chance of building a loyal clientele as well as some legitimate name recognition.

Consider a small company that makes high-end bicycle seats. It's a fairly niche market. They have the option of selling through a private label deal. Now, if they sell their high-end seats through that larger parent company, they will see their seats in every Target, Wal-Mart, and Sports Authority from coast to coast. What they cannot do, however, is market on the higher quality of their product. It just becomes another bike seat on a wall of bike seats; it's an expensive seat too. Even though your volume of sales will increase, your price point will be so close to cost, and your sales will be so limited due to competition, that you will not realize your full potential.

Consider the alternative. You build a brand synonymous with comfort, quality (whatever the most beneficial attributes of a bike seat are) and you allow that brand to take hold within the target market. People are willing to pay more, because they are an informed consumer that wants the best. Your product gains grassroots recognition and acclaim. Maybe you find a sponsorship deal with a pro that likes your product. Now, you are selling at a healthy price point (because people recognize quality) and your volume increases quarter to quarter. You may opt to invest some of that income into cheaper production (without compromising quality) or a marketing campaign, or further sponsorships, or a partnership. Or, at this point, you might allow a larger company to do some broadcast sales for you because now there's a brand identity and recognition will compel the casual shopper to pay the premium you ask.

If you are simply interested in moving the merchandise, then private label might be perfect for you. If you are in love with your own brand, uncompromising on profits or quality, or fear losing control of your 'baby', then you'll do much better to stay the course and remain private.

Chapter 4. How to Offer Value to a Larger Company

When considering opting to offer your product on a private label deal, you must consider what it is you are willing and able to offer the larger company. Don't expect them to offer much. Remember, they are already offering a lot. They offer you instant national exposure. They offer a broad and established client base who are as likely to purchase the name as they are the product. For these reasons, and other more practical economic matter, you are going to have to be ready to pull more than your weight when it comes to your new arrangement. In fact, in order to beat out your competitors when it comes to being accepted, you'll have to offer added value. There are a few ways you can do this.

Novelty versus Quality

Novelty is probably the best way to get your product optioned by a large company. This actually solves many headaches for both of you. By offering a novelty item, you remove the necessity of figuring out where it belongs. Found a new way to peel an apple? It goes in the utensils section, possibly as an endcap item. Develop a cleaner/degreaser? Perfect, put it in automotive, cleaning products, and paint aisles. You make some cutesy kids item and it goes in clothing or toys. You get the idea. You'll do volume sales just as an impulse buy, whether it be as a gift or a laugh. Don't underestimate the potential of a well known brand to move merchandise as a novelty.

Consider a company such as Sunbeam, or Farberware. We have come to associate them with clever kitchen gadgets (and more recently other genre as well). This is because we recognize them as a brand, but also we count on them offer innovative, if not always practical, novel products. New design features, new functionalities, a new twist on an old favorite, or a stab at a better mousetrap (not literally yet), and they have our attention. Many people will unknowingly peruse the kitchen tool section just looking for some clever new item that they haven't seen yet. This is likewise true for tools, toys, car and bicycle accessories, baby items, gardening gadgets, and of course electronics.

When a company builds part of its business model on providing new products in a constant stream, it's far cheaper and more efficient for them to contract other's ideas than it is to maintain a team of inventors and designers on retainer. What this means is that if your idea can go alongside an already established product line, then there's a good chance you have something worth writing a deal over.

The second area where you might tempt one of the big fish is if you offer superior quality. A known brand that wants to improve its image will often turn to an outside contract and private label it in order to add quality to their product line, without increasing their overhead with new facilities, research and development, or quality control. Think of what happened in the over the last twenty years with regard to generic brands.

Generic brands no longer exist in their former capacity. By and large, they have become 'store brands'. America's Choice, Smart Sense, Archer's Farms, and Kirkland are all store brands that acquire their products through private label deals. The perception of their quality has changed dramatically. In fact, in many blind consumer tests, the store brands actually fare better than their big-name counterparts. This makes sense, if we understand that a private label wholesaler has a greater interest in putting out a quality product. That is how they got in their position in the first place. They likely don't have the means to truly mass produce their product, and they don't yet have the network and resources to begin pulling lower quality components or ingredients from overseas sources. In short, for many private label vendors, their limitations are their strengths.

If you can offer a big name the opportunity to bolster their image by providing a quality product at a competitive price, then you've got a winning formula for success. Likewise, if you can help them maintain their image by providing something unique, that will sell also. But that's just the first step. It isn't enough to simply meet those parameters and then expect a big name to come knocking down your door. There's a bit more to the puzzle.

Chapter 5. Tempt Them, Hook Them, and Land Them

The first thing you'll need to do is to attract the interest of one of the big players in your market. In order to do this, you'll need a working functional prototype ,or sample. It should have been rigorously tested, and you should have the means to support any claims you make. With this substantive expression of your idea, you are unlikely to even get your foot in the door.

Before you go out showing off your brilliant new concept, you may (if you have the means) want to procure a series of patents for your particular device and/or components. This can be costly, but it will offer a margin of protection once you start playing in the big leagues. Of course, idea theft is always a possibility, and unless you have a million dollar retainer with a Manhattan law firm, you probably don't have the pockets to go blow for blow with a major company should a patent dispute arise. Unfortunately, this is just one of the risks of being the little guy. Your best defense is to move quickly, establish yourself in your field, and hope that if that fateful day does arrive, you've carved out a sustainable niche that will keep your business going (or that you get to sell your idea for millions and move on to the next project).

With private label deals, the company is unlikely to offer you any guarantee of advertising or marketing. As such, you should already have several concepts developed before you start your conversation.

Packaging

Actually go through with this. Design a package that is cheap and effective for your product. Pay attention to lettering, color schemes, displayability. One great way to get outstanding design is to get in touch with college students studying commercial design. They may work for free, or for very cheap. They have the unbridled enthusiasm to really give your package some zing.

You will want to write up a business synopsis of the packaging, including sourcing, weight, cost-in-bulk, etc in case the company decides they want to expand distribution. Likewise, you'll want to do the same with endcap displays and floor displays. Really the more complete your project seems, from production to point of sale, the more likely they will be to option your idea.

Marketing and Sourcing

Again, don't expect much help in this department either. Most big names figure that just appearing on the shelves is enough. It's no big deal to them if the product doesn't sell, they haven't invested much in you and they'll just discontinue the purchase. Therefore, it's up to you to get the word out. Promotional tricks, leafleting, and other standard marketing practices will help, but nothing works better than face to face. Appear at trade shows, business leaders forums, or any other event where you can put a face to your product, and put your product in front of someone's face. This will give you a chance to build contacts. In this manner, you may either spin your private label deal into a new venue, or possibly be able to parallel sell your item under two names.

As a manufacturer, you may not choose to private label under contract with a major company. What you may do instead is to offer your products piecemeal to a global market that may want your product. This is essentially the business model of companies like Alibaba, Manufacturers Global Resources, B2B Marketplace, DIY Trade, and Busy Trade Manufacturer

Directory, which all offer you the potential to list your product as well as to find wholesale suppliers. The internet is swarming with sites offering product sourcing and it seems there are more each day. You may find a ton of such sites just by making a Google search. These are like eBay sites for manufacturers and distributors. Some sites handle their own shipping and sales, some are list sites, and some are clearinghouses for other companies. Basically it's an immense world where you have limitless opportunities to hock your product on the global market. Chances are your design plans will be stolen almost immediately, but if your item isn't too especially unique, you won't be losing much. The rewards can be substantial if you land one major, or many minor contracts. The risks include design piracy, customs complications, and sketchy contract deals. You may not want to make this your first option, but that depends on how much of a risk taker you are; the money is certainly there to be made.

Production

Here is another area where many newcomers put themselves in a bind. When you do your first production run, done undershoot it. Typically there are various price breaks as you purchase higher quantities. Most experts recommend you purchase *a minimum* of 500 units for your initial run. Many say to have 1,000 either on hand, or close at hand. The reason for this is simple, and you can liken it to the whole breaking eggs to make an omelet thing.

In the beginning you need to promote. –and promote – and promote – and promote. Part of this is going to mean sending merchandise out to vendors, retailers, trade shows, business conferences, non-franchise entities; basically anyone who might possibly begin to turn sales for you. If the big name you decide to work with sees that you have a serious production flow already in place, they will shelve your product more aggressively. If numbers are the name of the game (and they are) then you have to be ready to hit the ground running.

If you are not in a position to scale production to that level, perhaps private label isn't for you yet. You can always work the artisanal markets until you find someone willing to float the costs of a contract production facility. And if your personal product just doesn't scale well (Aunty Jane's Persimmon Preserves) try building yourself a stable base of loyal purchasers. Some things just aren't meant to go global.

Basically, if you hope to land a contract with one of the heavy hitters, be prepared to do much of the work yourself. Be prepared to lose autonomy over time (not necessarily), and be prepared to enter the game with a full business plan; this includes all numbers and figures, possibilities for upscaling, packaging, marketing, contacts in the industry, and valuation and growth models. This is the first step into the world of the professionals, and you're not the only one looking to get noticed. Do your homework, do your legwork, and do your calculator work. It just might pay off big.

Chapter 6. Additional Marketing Tips

Parallel Sales

This is a concept worth considering. Basically what it amounts to is selling your product under two labels. One, through your private label contract, and the other through your own personal label. Now, different arrangements have differing legal stipulations, and we aren't about to get into a discussion of contract law. It is entirely up to you to research your contract, research state and federal laws, and decide if this is a strategy that's right for you. BUT – if you do decide to sell independently, there are a few ways to go about it.

Before you do anything though, be sure to repackage your product completely. You want the opportunity to grow independent brand recognition and value. Private label is great for volume, but bad on margin, and also offers little in the way of guarantees. If you are able to simultaneously build brand awareness of your product under your own private brand, that offers some excellent advantages.

Non-franchise Retail

You can direct market your product to stores that are less than national. Either you can contact their sales and marketing team (if they are big enough to have one) or go to the headquarters in person. Either way, you'll still want to have all your numbers crunched, T's crossed, and be prepared with a polished, professional pitch.

When considering markets for your product, think like a consumer. If you are trying to sell original, all natural, pure Vermont maple syrup, then don't try to sell it in Vermont. Establish a market in an area that doesn't have access to such a localized luxury item. You'll see increased sales, and also be able to charge a premium. Before you go meeting with potential buyers, have a full plan of how you'll ship the product and ensure a steady product flow. Have an emergency backup to cover unexpected booms in sales. Prepare for the *best*, and your buyers will have confidence in you.

Likewise, you may not be able to market your new bicycle shocks in Kansas. Are their serious cyclists there? Of course. But you're going to do much better in a market familiar with buying high-end tools and toys for their hobby. Take it to Colorado and spend a week on the road. Do your research before you head out and consider giving some product away to cycling clubs, tour agencies, bike shops, etc. Think big and make a big impression.

Online Sales

Of course you should have a professional quality website up and running; that's obvious. But let's consider our options for direct sales over the internet. If you can simultaneously build brand awareness through your direct marketing campaign, and then feature your product on the nations number-one e-commerce retail site (eBay, Amazon FBA) then customers don't have to work so hard to find you.

Amazon FBA

While eBay is pretty straight forward, it's going to get left in the dust by Amazon FBA. This is an all around platform for peer-to-peer sales. The best thing about Amazon FBA is that you don't have to worry about shipping, guarantees, or not getting paid.

The way it works is that you create a membership (free personal, or pay professional). You then list your items for sale. You choose which category the item belongs in, and list it there. You create a TITLE (use all caps it's more effective), and then you give a product description. Here's a good place to reference the communities where you did your most thorough marketing, any endorsements you have, and what makes your product special.

Once you have your listing posted, you say how many of that item you want to stock. Let's say you stock 50 of your innovative baby bottles (because that's how many you can fit in a single box). This next part is the coolest. You individually package your items, and throw them in one single box! You print the shipping label from the Amazon FBA website, and you mail the whole thing to one of Amazon's regional warehouses. They take care of inventorying and storing your products while you wait for the sales to roll in. When someone places an order through Amazon, the warehouse picks, packs, and ships your product. Done deal. All you have to do is make any pricing adjustments you see necessary, keep your stock up at Amazon, and focus on marketing. That way, you can ship samples all over the country, and they can order as many as you maintain in stock, with Amazon's 2 day guarantee for shipping anywhere in the lower 48 states.

This is nothing short of revolutionary. Now, of course Amazon takes a nice bite out of your sales, but with a bit of quick math you can find a price point that works and go from there. Imagine not having to store, package, and ship your own product. Plus, you get to take advantage of Amazon's partnership with companies like UPS both when they ship to the client and when you ship to the warehouse.

The Amazon website offers all kinds of tips for creating a better page, but most is common sense. The most important thing is to get your product listed. If it isn't listed it can't sell. And this model costs you next to nothing. Biggest online retailer in the world, free storage, 2 day guaranteed shipping, name recognition, guaranteed payment; truly this is a revolution in the making.

Conclusion

So now you have the basics for selling your own product. Team up with the pros, play small ball and grow into big profits, or take the hybrid route through Amazon FBA; grass roots marketing with professional product handling. Stick with one, or try all three. It's time for your dream to come true.